Isaac Allerton, first assistant of Plymouth colony

Patten, Edwin Beaman, 1835- [from old catalog]

ISAAC ALLERTON.

First Assistant of Plymouth Colony

E. B. PATTEN, Compiler

1908

Press of
IMPERIAL PRINTING CO.
MINNEAPOLIS

NOTE.

Mr. Walter S. Allerton, in the "Allerton Genealogy" has outlined what the writer has endeavored roughly to fill in, viz.: A defense of Isaac Allerton's name and fame from the charges and insinuations against his good faith and integrity made by Gov. William Bradford in his History.

If any find patience to read this account of an ancient controversy, he hopes that his lack of skill in arranging and presenting the case may not prevent their taking an impartial view of the evidence.

With little opinion of the fairness of Bradford as a historian, or of his abilities as a business manager, the writer has neither intention nor desire to disparage the courage and political tact which enabled the governor to lead Plymouth colony through its early years of poverty, weakness and dissension, to better and more stable conditions.

It is only with his injustice and jealousy, which left a legacy of detraction to be administered upon two hundred years later, that the writer has any quarrel.

E. B. PATTEN,

Minneapolis, Minn.
Aug. 8, 1908.

ISAAC ALLERTON

His connection with Plymouth Colony, with some
comments on Bradfords History

Isaac Allerton, the first Assistant (Dep. Gov.) of Plymouth Colony, has left us no clue to his birthplace or ancestry. One of his descendants reports that he was born in the northeastern part of England about 1583, and was apprenticed to a tailor of London in his youth, but quotes no authority for these statements.

We know that a sister, Sarah Allerton, married John Vincent of London, and it is probable that the Allerton family were living in that city in the first years of the seventeenth century. Our first record of Isaac Allerton is as a merchant in Leyden, and as a member of the English church there, under Robinson's pastoral charge. Whether he was with this body during their brief stay in Amsterdam is uncertain, but he probably joined the colony in Holland about the year 1609.

He prospered during his residence in Holland, for he was made a freeman of the city of Leyden, February 7, 1614, a considerable honor, conferred on but two others of the English colony; and at the time of the emigration to New England he was reputed the wealthiest member of the colony, and was one of the heaviest stocktakers in the company.

The means to fit out the emigrants, and provide for their transportation and subsistence, were raised only in part among themselves in Holland and England, the remainder being furnished by some seventy adventurers (as they were termed) of London, who were to hold title to the lands and property of the company, and share in the profits of the enterprise if any there should be, after a term of years.

The negotiation for this money proceeded slowly, with a great deal of discussion, and much quarreling and dissension, but articles of agreement were finally signed, and a ship, the "Speedwell," fitted out. She sailed from Delft-Haven August 1, 1620, for South Hampton, Eng., where she was joined by the "Mayflower" from London. The "Speedwell" proved unseaworthy—her passengers were transferred to the "Mayflower," and after many delays the little ship found her way across the Atlantic, casting anchor in Cape Cod Harbor November 21st.

Some discontent and insubordination arising among the emigrants, the leaders called a meeting in the cabin of the "Mayflower," and drew up the celebrated "Compact of the Pilgrim Fathers." This was signed by 41 of the passengers: Carver, Bradford, Winslow and Brewster were the first four signers, Allerton the fifth.

After some exploration of the coast, the memorable landing at Plymouth was made, and the Pilgrims realized for the first time the terrible hardships of a pioneer settlement on the bleak New England coast, in the fiercest months of the year.

Weakened by the crowding and confinement of the ship, and by scanty and unwholesome food, they were in poor case to endure the privation and exposure which followed. In a few months the resulting sickness carried off half their number.

Isaac Allerton's wife died among the first, on February 25, 1621. He had married her in Leyden, the record in the Stadt-Huis, where marriages are recorded, giving "Mary "Norris, a maid from Newberry, Eng., and Isaac Allerton, "young man, of London, Eng." This notice, or publication, was October 4, 1611, and the marriage was November 4, 1611. By her he had four children, all born in Leyden, a son, Bartholomew, and three daughters, Mary, Remember and Sarah. The latter did not come in the Mayflower, but remained in Leyden with her aunt, Mrs. Priest, coming over with her a year or two later.

In April Gov. Carver died and Bradford was chosen governor and Allerton "assistant," or deputy governor, an office which he held several years. Bradford's journal says: "In March following, (1621) Mr. Allerton with Capt. Standish 'went venturously' to treat with Massasoit." In September, 1621, a party was sent to visit the Massachusetts Bay Indians, and named the first headland of Nantasket for their deputy governor, "Point Allerton," which name it still bears.

The colony, so inauspiciously begun, struggled along for some five years, burdened with debt, and at times suffering greatly for needed supplies: the London adventurers, who made the first advances for the outfitting of the emigrants, having refused to supply the company with more money, or goods. In 1625 Capt. Standish was sent to England with instructions to make some composition with the adventurers, but returned without having effected anything.

In 1626 Allerton was sent over to make the best arrangement he could with the London people, and also to borrow, if possible, money to supply necessaries for the colony. For this purpose he had a power of attorney from three or four of the leading colonists.

He succeeded in getting some money and sent home the needed supplies. He also arranged with the adventurers to transfer to him (Allerton) and such others of the colonists as he should think fit to join with him, all the rights that the adventurers had to the lands and property held by the company for the sum of £1,800, this sum to be paid in annual installments of £200, the first payment to be made in 1628.

This agreement was to be ratified by the planters by the return ship. This was the turning point in the struggle of the colony for existence. The debt thus compromised was about £7,000, and the adventurers held title to all the land, houses and goods that the colonists had in their possession. Until these claims were in some way cleared off, it was not possible to secure the needed supplies to keep the settlement alive.

Allerton was sent, as Bradford says, because he was better qualified by his business experience and education than any other, to transact this business and because he had "good acceptation" with their London friends and creditors. The agreement with the adventurers was signed the 15th of November, 1626.

On Allerton's return the agreement was submitted to the Plymouth people and approved. The colonists, or the majority of them, then took shares in this purchase, each head of a family and each unmarried man being allowed to take one share and the former to take in addition one share for each member of his family, each shareholder to be responsible for any deficit that might arise (from the profit of the trade of the company being insufficient to discharge the obligations incurred by the purchase) in proportion to the number of shares held. The trade of the colony in fish, furs, timber, etc., to be carried on for the benefit of the purchasers.

This matter of buying the claims of the London creditors having been decided, before they sent Allerton back to England to ratify the agreement, Bradford says, "Some of "the chief men among the planters deliberated privately. "Not only how they might discharge those great engage-

"ments which lay so heavily upon them, but also, how they
"might (if possibly they could) devise means to help some
"of their friends and brethren at Leyden over unto them,
"who desired so much to come to them, and they desired
"so much their company."

"To effect which, they resolved to run a high course,
"and of great adventure, not knowing otherwise how to
"bring it about."

"Which was, to hire the trade of the company for cer-
"tain years, and in that time to undertake to pay that
" £1,800 and all the rest of the debts that then lay on the
"plantation, which was about £600 more, and so to set
"them free, and to return the trade to the generalitie again
"at the end of the term."

Bradford continues: "They called the company to-
"gether, stated what the debts were, and the terms upon
"which this new partnership would agree to clear them, in
"a certain time, etc."

"But their other ends (i. e., the bringing over of the
"Leyden people) they were fain to keep secret, having only
"acquainted privately some trusty friends; who were glad
"of the same, but doubted how they would be able to per-
"form it."

The company (i. e., those who had just taken shares in
the purchase of the adventurers' rights) after some discussion agreed with the new partnership as follows, viz.:

The company sold to Bradford, Standish and Allerton,
and such other parties as these should see fit to take as
partners, all the boats, the pinnace, all tools and imple-
ments, and all the stock of merchandise and furs that were
then in the company's possession.

They also agreed that the new partnership was to have
for six years the whole trade in furs and merchandise, with
all the privileges therof, "as the said colony doth now, or
"may, use the same." The term of the trade to begin on
the last of September, then next ensuing.

And they also agreed that each holder of a share in the
company should pay annually to the partnership three
bushels of corn, or six pounds of tobacco, as the partners
might elect.

In consideration of which the partnership agreed to
discharge, and acquit the colony of all debts due at the date
of this agreement, whether for the purchase money due
the adventurers or other outstanding claims against the
colony. The partners also agreed to bring over annually
during the term of this agreement shoes and hose to the

amount of £50, to be sold to the colonists for corn at 6s. a bushel. At the end of six years the whole trade to return to the use of the colony.

Mr. Allerton returned to London to close up the purchase with the adventurers, taking a copy of the agreement between the colonists and the new partnership with him, with instruction from his Plymouth partners to endeavor to interest some of his, and their, special friends in London in their enterprises, viz.: the trading venture, and "the "bringing over some of their friends from Leyden as they "should be able."

"In which enterprise" (I am quoting Bradford) "if any "of their London friends would join with them, they should "thankfully accept of their love and partnership herein."

He had also instructions from his partners to procure, if possible, a patent for a trading district on the Kennebec river for their exclusive use; for Bradford says, "The "Piscataway people threatened to procure a patent, and "so shut out the Plymouth people" from that trade. On his arrival in England, he closed the bargain with the adventurers and gave them the partnerships bonds for the payment of the £1,800 agreed upon.

He obtained from the council for New England the patent desired on the Kennebec. He also induced four of their London friends to become partners with them in their purchase of the trade of the colony, thus securing the necessary financial support, without which their scheme must have failed. This partnership, as finally made up, consisted of eight of the colonists, viz., Bradford, Standish, Allerton, Winslow, Brewster, Howland, Alden and Prence, and four of London, viz., James Shirley, John Beauchamp, Richard Andrews and Timothy Hatherley.

Shirley, who seems to have been the leading spirit of the London end of this partnership, was a goldsmith (the equivalent of a modern banker). He writes to the Plymouth partners a letter, which Bradford quotes, as follows:

"It is true, as you write, that your engagements are "great: not only the purchase, but you are necessitated to "take up (i. e., borrow) the stock you work upon, and that "not at 6 or 8 per ct., as it is here let out, but at 30, 40, "yea and some at 50 per ct., which, were not your gains "great, and God's blessing on your honest endeavors more "than ordinary, it could not be that you should long sub-"sist in the maintaining and upholding of your worldly "affairs: and this your honest and discreet agent, Mr. Al-"lerton, hath seriously considered, and deeply laid to mind "how to ease you of it   *   *   *   "

"I also see by your letter you desire I shall be your
"agent, or factor here.* * * Now, because I am sickly,
"and we are all mortal, I have advised Mr. Allerton to
"join Mr. Beauchamp with me in your deputation (i. e.,
"agency) which I conceive to be very necessary and good
"for you."

With this letter of Shirley's was sent a full and com-
prehensive power of attorney, authorizing and deputing
James Shirley and John Beauchamp to receive and dispose
of all goods sent to England from Plymouth by the partners, and consigned to them, or either of them, in any
manner, and on any terms they, or either of them, shall
think best. To buy and ship to New England to the partners all goods that shall be thought fit by them or either of
them. To receive, collect or compound any debts that may
be due the partnership; and generally to do and perform
any and all acts that may be necessary for the transac-
tion of their business. In short, as strong and full a power
as could be drawn. This document was executed by the
Plymouth partners, November 18, 1627, and returned to
Mr. Shirley.

In the fall of 1628 Allerton returned to Plymouth and
brought, Bradford says, "Some goods of his own and sold
"them, which was looked on with some jealousy by his
"partners at Plymouth." "But," he continues, "they re-
"solved to send him to England this year (1629) consider-
"ing how well he had done the former business, and what
"good acceptation he had with their friends there. As,
'also, seeing sundry of their friends from Leyden were
"sent for, which would, or might be, much further ed by his
"means." "Again, seeing the patent for the Kennebec must
"be enlarged, by reason of the former mistake in bounding
"it, and it was conceived, in a manner, the same charge
"would serve to enlarge this at home (i. e., the Plymouth
"patent) with it, and he, that had begun the former last
"year, would be the fittest to effect this."

Allerton went over to England (probably later in the
year) for Shirley writes to the governor under date March
19, 1630 (N. S.):

"Some of your letters I received in July and some since
"by Mr. Pierce, but till our main business, the patent, was
"granted, I could not settle my mind, nor pen, to writing."

"Mr. Allerton was so turmoiled about it, as, verily, I
"could not, nor would not, have undergone it if I might
"have had a thousand pounds; but the Lord so blessed
"his labors (even beyond expectation in these evil days)
"as he obtained the love and favor of great men in repute
"and place."

"He got granted from the Earl of Warwick and Sir
"Ferdinando Gorges all that Mr. Winslow desired in his
"letters to me, and more also, which I leave to him to
"relate."

"Then he sued to the king to confirm their grant, and
"to make you a corporation, and so enable you to make
"and execute laws in such large and ample manner as the
"Massachusetts plantation hath it: which the king
"graciously granted, referring to the Lord Keeper to give
"order to the solicitor to draw it up, if there were a prece-
"dent for it."

"So the Lord Keeper furthered it all he could and also
"the solicitor, but as Festus said to Paul, 'with no small
"sum of money obtained I this freedom' for by the way
"many riddles must be resolved, and many locks must be
"opened with the silver, nay, the golden.key."

"Then it came to the Lord Treasurer to have his war-
"rant for freeing the customs for a certain time: but he
"would not do it, but referred it to the council table—and
"there Mr. Allerton attended, day by day, when they sat,
"but could not get his petition read.

"And by reason of Mr. Pierce his staying with all the
"passengers at Bristol, he (Mr. Allerton) was forced to
"leave the further prosecuting of it to a solicitor. But
"there is no fear, or doubt, that it will be granted, for he
"hath the chief of them to friend, yet it will be marvelously
"needful for him to return by the first ship that comes
"from thence, for, if you had this confirmed then were you
"complete, and might bear such sway and government, as
"were fit for your rank and place that God hath called you
"unto; and stop the mouth of base and scurrilous fellows,
"that are ready to question and threaten you in every action
"you do.

"And besides, if you have the customs free for 7 years
"inward, and 21 years outward, the charge of the patent
"will soon be recovered, and there is no fear of obtaining it.
"But such things must come by degrees. Men cannot
"hasten it, as they would; wherefore, we (I write in behalf
"of all my partners here) desire you to be earnest with Mr.
"Allerton to come, and his wife to spare him this one year
"more to finish this great and weighty business which we
"conceive to be much for your good and, I hope, for your
"posteritie and many generations to come."

Bradford comments on this: "It was afterward appre-
"hended that the main reason the business of the patent
"was not concluded this year was that Mr. Allerton's policy

"was to postpone it, that he might again be sent over to "conclude it."

This seems an ungrateful and uncharitable view to take, in the light of Shirley's letters, and of Allerton's strenuous and seemingly unappreciated labors for the colony, but another incident set down by Bradford undoubtedly had much to do with the trouble which now began between the partners. One Morton, who had been sent back to England by the Massachusetts authorities a year previously as an "undesirable citizen," was a passenger in the ship on which Allerton returned, and on arrival at Plymouth was employed by Allerton as a secretary, or clerk. This gave great offense to some of the leading men, Standish in particular, who had assisted in the former arrest of Morton.

Then (Bradford goes on) Allerton had made some money while in England on some private ventures, and had brought over goods which were not ordered by the Plymouth folk. In short, there seems to have been a great jealousy of Allerton, lest he might use his opportunities while in England to help his private means, though it nowhere appears in Bradford's statement that he did so in any way to the detriment of his partners in Plymouth, or London.

As to the charge of exceeding his instructions in amount of goods brought over, Bradford says that Allerton excused himself from that, and laid the blame, if any there was, on Shirley and the London partners. Recalling the unlimited power given Shirley and Beauchamp two years before and still unrevoked, this seems to have been a complete answer. In fact, Bradford admits that Allerton referred them to Shirley's letters for the reasons for the shipments, and says, "Indeed, Mr. Shirley wrote things tending this way, but "it is like he was overruled by Mr. Allerton, and harkened "more to him than to their letters from hence."

What a fair minded, just old fellow the governor was! He continues: "But another and more secret cause kept "them from complaining of Allerton's course:" that was his having married Elder Brewster's daughter, and they "were loth to grieve or offend their beloved Elder and so "bore with much in that respect."

In the same letter of March 19, 1630, N. S., Shirley urges Bradford to push the trading—that the time of their purchase will soon be gone and others will step in. He tells him that he and Mr. Beauchamp have obtained a patent for a trading district on the Penobscot and have outfitted one Ashley to occupy it, and offers to take the Plymouth people as partners in this venture, if they desire to join in it. He explicitly says:

"Mr. Allerton had no power from you to make this new "contract, neither was he willing to do anything therein "without your consent and approbation." The Plymouth folk feared it might offend the London partners if they refused to join them in this scheme, and wrote them that they would accept their offer and join in the venture on the Penobscot. After the fishing season this year (1629) was over Mr. Allerton found a bargain in a cargo of salt at a fishing station and bought it for about £113, and could have sold it shortly after for £30 clear profit, but "Mr. "Winslow coming that way from the Kennebec stayed Mr. "Allerton from selling it, and the partners resolved to keep "it, and send out a vessel from the west coast of England "fishing the next season."

This, from Bradford, shows that a fishing vessel was intended by the Plymouth people to be bought or hired in England, and that the sending of the "Friendship" the next spring was not a surprise to them as alleged by Bradford later.

In the fall of 1630 Allerton was again sent to London. Bradford says: "Upon consideration of the business about "the patent, and in what state it was left, and Mr. Shirley's "earnest pressing to have Mr. Allerton come over again to "finish it, and perfect the accounts, etc., it was concluded "to send him over this year again, though it was with some "fear and jealousy. Yet he gave them fair words, and "promises of well performing their business according to "their direction, and to mend his former errors."

It is hard to conjecture exactly what errors Allerton promised to "amend," unless it were the harboring and employment of Morton.

The same ship that carried Allerton back to England this year took letters from the Plymouth folk leaving the London partners to decide whether or not to send over a ship for fishing, only desiring that if one were sent she should bring some trading goods.

There were no letters, Bradford says, for many months from Allerton or Shirley, but at last came a letter from Shirley "which made them much to marvel thereat." This letter stated that the London people had "this year set forth "a fishing ship, and a trading ship, which latter we have "bought, and so have disbursed a great deal of money, as "may and will appear by the accounts." And because this ship was intended both for trading and fishing, Mr. Hatherley was to go over in her to assist, if necessary. Mr. Allerton, and also to get a full account of the business of the partnership. Shirley begs the Plymouth people to entertain Mr. Hatherley kindly, and to give him all information as to the state of the business.

This trading ship of which Mr. Shirley writes was called the "White Angel." The London partners thought her necessary to supply the stations which the partnership had established on the Penobscot and Kennebec rivers, and, though the bills of sale of the vessel were taken in the name of the London partners, Shirley writes that they had no thought of dividing in anything from their Plymouth partners. In another letter he says that Allerton had told him that unless a ship were bought Ashley could not be supplied, and unless he were supplied "we could not be satisfied what we "were out for you, and further, he gave some reasons, "which we spare to relate, unless by your unreasonable re- "fusal you will force us, and so hasten that fire, which is "kindling too fast already."

The differences between the partners were brought to an open rupture by this dispute about the "White Angel," and the losses made by the fishing vessel, the "Friendship." Allerton left the partnership, Bradford says "being dismissed," but probably he left at his own motion, for Bradford afterward complains that Allerton, having got them "among the briers," has now deserted them and left them to get out alone. Bradford sums up his complaints against Allerton (p. 285 of the 1856 Ed. of his History) as follows: "I shall not need to be large therein, doing it here, once "for all:

"First. It seems to appear clearly that Ashley's busi- "ness and the buying of this ship (the White Angel) and "the courses framed thereon were first contrived and pro- "posed by Mr. Allerton, as also the pleas and pretenses "which he made of the inability of the plantation to repay "their moneys, etc., and the hopes he gave them of doing "it with profit, was more believed and relied on by them "(the London partners) than anything the plantation did "or said."

"Second. It is like, though Mr. Allerton might think "not, to wrong the plantation in the main, yet his own gain "and private ends led him aside in these things; for it "came to be known and I have it in a letter under Mr. Shir- "ley's hand, that in the first two or three years of his em- "ployment he had cleared up £400 and put it into a brew "house of Mr. Collier's of London, at first under Mr. Shir- "ley's name, etc., besides what he might have otherwise."

"Again, Mr. Shirley and he had particular dealings in "some things: for he had bought up the beaver that sea- "men and other passengers had brought over to Bristol, "and at other places, and charged the bills to London, which "Mr. Shirley paid; and they got sometimes £50 apiece in "a bargain, as was made known by Mr. Hatherley and oth- "ers, besides what might be otherwise; which might make "Mr. Shirley harken unto him in many things.

"And yet, I believe as he (Shirley) in his fore-mentioned "letter writes, he would never side in any particular trade "which would be conceived wrong the plantation, and eat "up and destroy the general" (i. e., the company).

In his third specification Bradford intimates that the London partners having done so much for the plantation previously, thought there might be an opportunity for profit in buying these two ships (the "Friendship" and "White Angel") and sending them over, but, finding a loss prob- able, had charged them to the general account, "feeling" (the Gov. says) "it was more meet for the plantation to "bear the loss than they who had lost so much already."

In the dispute about the "White Angel" Shirley said that Allerton approved the purchase, as agent for the Ply- mouth end of the partnership. The only power of attorney ever mentioned as given to Allerton was one authorizing him to borrow money for supplies in 1626, before the pur- chase of the adventurers' rights. That was a personal and individual authority for the specific purpose of borrowing some £200, and was lodged in Mr. Shirley's hands at the time the money was borrowed, as a security, and was never, so far as appears, heard of again.

At any rate, so far as creating any liability of the new partnership goes, it was mere waste paper, but this Brad- ford seems to have overlooked.

The power given to Shirley & Beauchamp was suffi- cient to hold the partners for any expenditure, however extravagant, that was in the way of their trade. As to the Ashley business, Bradford certainly was losing his memory of events when he wrote that paragraph, for Shirley pro- posed their joining with them (the London people) in this venture, and distinctly says that Allerton had no power to go into such a venture for his partners and would do noth- ing in it without their consent and approbation. And the governor says they joined in it for fear their London friends would be offended if they declined.

So far as the governor's second charge is at all worthy of notice, it is refuted by his own statement at its close. Allerton certainly had a right to any gain he could make in any dealing that did not injure or compete with his partnership business, and Bradford says he does not believe he would do anything in a "particular" or private deal that would "eat up and destroy the general".

His third count is directed rather at Shirley and Beauchamp than at Allerton, and needs no refutation here.

His last complaint is more serious. He says that when Allerton retired from the partnership he claimed that they owed him some £300, while the partnership (i. e., the Plymouth end) claimed that he owed them £2,000. A part of this was a claim for a part of the cargo of the "White Angel," which the Plymouth people refused to receive, or to pay for, and which was sold by Hatherley, acting for the London partners, to Allerton, after he had terminated his connection with the partnership. Allerton was bound by his bargain to pay the price of these goods to Shirley & Beauchamp, for whom and himself Hatherley was acting, and the Plymouth people having refused to accept, or to pay for, these goods, certainly had no right to the payment from Allerton. This, however, was but a small part of the difference between their claims. The great divergence in the accounts may perhaps not appear so wonderful if we refer to Bradford's story of the attempt to adjust the accounts with the London partners five years later.

He says (p. 347) that "Beauchamp & Andrews com-
"plained that though each of them were out about £1,100
"since 1631 that now (in 1636) they had not received a
"penny, but that all furs, etc., had been sent to Mr. Shirley
"who still desired to draw money from them—and blamed
"them because they would not advance it. They (the Plymouth folk) marveled much at this," for they had consigned furs to England in that time, which they thought to be of the value of over £10,000, and had no invoice of goods shipped them, nor account sales of furs.

In fact, from the beginning the bookkeeping at the Plymouth end seems to have been of the loosest and most careless sort, if, indeed, one can call it bookkeeping, where no books are kept.

No invoices of goods received from London, nor accounts of furs, etc., sold for their account in London seem to have been received, or if received, preserved.

In 1631 Shirley sent over to Plymouth a young man (a younger brother of Winslow) as an accountant for them. He had proposed to send one the year before, but the Plymouth people were unwilling to be at this charge. This year, however, Josias Winslow came over, and they employed him.

Now (in 1636) they tried to reckon up their liabilities and assets, and found they had nothing to show, either what they had had from England, nor what they owed.

Bradford says (p. 347): "But it may be objected, How "comes it that they could not as well exactly set down their "receipts as their returns, but thus estimate it? I answer, "Two things were the cause of it: The first and principal "was that the new accountant, which they in England "would needs press upon them, did wholly fail them, and "could never give them any account, but trusting to his "memory and to loose papers, let things run into such con-"fusion that neither he, nor any with him, could bring "things to rights.

"But being often called upon to perfect his accounts, "he desired to have such a time, and such a time of leisure, "and he would do it. .

"In the interim he fell into a great sickness, and in con-"clusion it fell out that he could make no account at all.

"His books were, after a little good beginning, left alto-"gether unperfect, and his papers, some were lost, and "others so confused, as he knew not what to make of them, "himself, when they came to be searched and examined.

"This was not unknown to Mr. Shirley, and they (the "Plymouth people) came to smart for it, to purpose, both "thus in England and also here.

"For they conceived they had lost some hundreds of "pounds for goods trusted out in the place, which were lost, "for want of clear accounts to call them in. Another reason "of this mischief was that after Mr. Winslow was sent to "England to demand accounts, and to except against the "'White Angel' they never had any price sent with their "goods nor any certain invoice of them, but all things stood "in confusion and they were fain to guess at the price of "them."

This astounding confession of carelessness, incompe-tence and stupidity, under Bradford's own hand, makes it rather unnecessary to refute any claim of indebtedness which has no better base to stand on than the evidence of the governor and his bookkeeper.

Why did not Bradford, or Winslow, or some of the other five Plymouth partners, discover this state of affairs before five years had elapsed?

Was Allerton the only one of the eight Plymouth men who could keep an account or prevent the business falling into this chaotic confusion?

When he retired from the firm, was the business given over to be looted by any who were near enough to the managers to get their hands in the till?

In these latter days that would be the inevitable conclusion. Were the Pilgrims better men than we? Perhaps; but there is little to show them so. Allerton may have been a speculative, and over sanguine business man, but he could hardly have made a worse mess of their affairs than they did. Winslow was "sent into England to demand accounts" (in 1632), says Bradford. Well! Why didn't he get them? And why was it that from that time "they never had any price sent with their goods, nor any "certain invoice of them, but all things stood in confusion, "and they were fain to guess at the price of them"? Winslow was governor in 1633 and 1636, Prence in 1634, Bradford in 1635. The delinquent bookkeeper was Winslow's brother. Is there anything in Allerton's record, one-half as bad as this flagrant neglect and mismanagement of the affairs of the firm?

Yet not a word from Bradford against Winslow's good faith. His creed was all right. He had not harbored the Godless Morton, nor extended a friendly hand to Roger Williams.

After Allerton's connection with the partnership ceased, he began trading and fishing on the eastern coast on his own account.

He became, thus, a competitor to his former partners, and the hostile feeling growing out of their former disagreements became stronger in the governor's mind. He complains that Allerton sold goods on credit to traders on the Maine coast, and thus injured the Plymouth trade.

Why should not Allerton sell to whom he pleased? Did he owe his old partners any consideration? He had been with them in Holland for years, had put his money in with theirs in the outfitting of the Speedwell and the Mayflower. He had been an able and efficient worker in their first years in New England.

When the colony was in dire distress, and Standish had failed to secure any settlement with their creditors, Allerton was sent over, and by his diplomacy and business tact, persuaded the adventurers to accept the Agreement of Composition, which gave to the colonists for the first time the ownership of their homes, and a hope of maintaining their settlement in Plymouth.

He borrowed the money to supply their necessities, and to bring over more of their friends from Leyden. He procured the patent for the Kennebec district, also for the

Plymouth colony from the Council for New England.

He had spent his time and labor for years in traversing the ocean and exploring the dangerous coasts of Maine in their interest and behalf.

His reward was the jealous suspicion of his own partners, who would have driven him from the partnership he had created sooner had he not been the only one among them of any business capacity, who possessed the confidence of the London partners supplying the money to keep the concern going; and the jealous grumblers at Plymouth dared send no one else to England lest the supplies be stopped.

It seems plain enough to a reader of Bradford's History and Letter Book that the governor had his hands full in controlling the many little factions in the colony; and, with Standish's aid, in defending the colony from the incursions of the Indians.

He had little time, and less capacity, to give to the business affairs of the partnership. He was absolutely ignorant of their business and knew not whether there was profit or loss in it. The accounts with the London partners (which have been alluded to) ran for years without auditing, or settlement, and when finally made up, were, as might have been foreseen, hotly disputed, and were only adjusted, after long years of contention, by a compromise in which, as is quite usual, both parties claimed they were wronged. The London people, however, **knew** whether they were cheated, or not. The Plymouth people didn't. The seven partners who were the Plymouth end of the firm were the real rulers of the colony all through the years of these transactions, and enforced such rules and ordinances as they saw fit to make. These laws (if they can be so-called) stood by sufferance rather than by authority. The colony never had a charter from the king, and the government being self-constituted, the leaders were very much afraid of any reports to their prejudice reaching the ears of the English people or the English government.

They made no scruple of searching outgoing vessels for correspondence, nor of seizing and opening private letters, and gave easy belief to any rumor that fed their jealousy of all not disposed to submit to their dictation.

By keeping, as in the purchase business related by Bradford, their designs secret from the majority of the settlers, they succeeded for a long time in keeping the government of the colony in their own hands.

It will show how absolute Bradford felt their control of the situation was, to note how frequently he uses the term "Plantation" when he is referring only to the seven Plymouth partners. He constantly treats the "partners" as "the colony," though they were but seven men out of more than a hundred.

Allerton was less devoted to the rigid doctrines of the Separatists, and more liberal in his religious views, than most of his partners. His friendship with Roger Williams led to his leaving the colony about 1634, and later to his being requested to leave Massachusetts.

He had learned the lesson of toleration from the Dutchmen in Leyden, and had no mind for persecution of those who could not accept the narrow creed of the Separatists who dominated the colony.

His business education and experience acquired in London and Leyden, and in many voyages of trade and adventure had broadened his views and made him an "undesirable citizen" in the eyes of the bigots who controlled both the Massachusetts and Plymouth colonies.

Bradford's History was written nearly twenty years after these events. His memory is shown, by his frequent errors in fixing dates, etc., to have been at times at fault, but the great drawback to its value as original evidence in the case under discussion is the bitter prejudice against Allerton which is manifest throughout.

The governor was very human. His feelings colored his story, and makes it necessary for one who seeks the truth to allow liberally for the "personal equation." Bear in mind that this history is practically the only account we have of the years of this partnership. Allerton has not left us a word of his side of the story. Note, too, that in all the governor's complaining, he nowhere charges any positive dishonesty nor any specific act of bad faith against Allerton. It is all vague, such phrases as "It was conceived" and "It was apprehended"—mere surmise and innuendo—nowhere bold assertion.

So far as we can judge at this late day, the real trouble seems to have been (aside from the religious differences and the squabble about Morton) that Shirley and the London people were very anxious to increase the trade on the coast sufficiently to give a reasonable chance of recouping themselves for their advances before the partnership expired by limitation. They had by far the larger investment in the company, and if Allerton did to some extent agree with their views rather than with Bradford's and Winslow's, it is certainly no reason to accuse him of bad faith.

When losses, through the fishing and trading ventures of 1631, occurred, the Plymouth folk were what gamblers call "bad losers," and sought a scapegoat to lay the blame upon.

Shirley was the one who had all the power and responsibility (vested in him by the act of the Plymouth people, when they could see no other way out of their troubles) and should take all the blame, if blame there be. He, perhaps, did not treat them fairly after Allerton left them, but if he did take any unfair advantage of their business stupidity and ignorance, he was obliged to forego some part of his gains, for they did not settle his claim till many years after, and then at a discount.

After Allerton left the colony, in 1634, he met with many losses. The French destroyed a trading station and a large stock of goods which he had at Machios. Many of his fishing vessels were lost at sea, and fortune seemed to have deserted all his enterprises.

With his usual fairness, Bradford attributes these disasters to the "judgment of God," but does not refer the terrible sickness and misfortune which befell the colony in its first years to the same inscrutable cause. Had Allerton left us from his own hand as full an account of all these years as we have from the governor's, it is quite possible that so different a picture would be presented as to place Allerton, the merchant, the liberal, the exile, in higher estimation as a founder of New England and a defender of religious liberty, than even the pious governor. But the records of his achievements are buried in the London account books, the archives of the colonial boards, and the state papers of England.

The factions and jealousies in the colony, the doubts of his orthodoxy, and the absence of any record from a less jaundiced historian than Bradford have prevented his receiving the credit that was his due, for his distinguished services to the colony of Plymouth. The scanty mention of his personal actions in the early records gives us glimpses of a kindly and generous man.

When his brother-in-law, Godbertson, died insolvent, about 1633, the administrator of the estate reported to the court that, though he was the largest creditor, "Mr. Aller-"ton would not claim any part of his debt, preferring to lose "all rather than others should lose any."

He succored the shipwrecked many times, at his trading stations, and extended a helping hand, whenever needed, to his connections and neighbors.

His personality impressed strongly those around him—whether the citizens of Leyden, the court officials at ██████. *White*hall, the merchants of London, the rough traders on the Maine coast, the burghers of New Amsterdam or his neighbors at Plymouth and New Haven.

In 1634, two years after his retirement from the partnership, he was chosen by the freemen of Plymouth an "Assistant," which would certainly indicate that he was still in good standing with the mass of the colonists there.

In 1643 while in New Amsterdam he was chosen one of a "committee for council and advice" on public affairs—really a "steering committee" for Gov. Kieft, who had entirely lost the confidence and respect of the citizens.

In all these various associations he was always a man amongst men, vital, forceful, hopeful. That this man who had given so much of his life, so much of his substance, to the founding and sustaining of Plymouth settlement, was in the smallest degree unfaithful to any of his obligations to his townsmen, or his partners, seems incredible.

No mere surmise can smirch such a record. Evidence to such purpose must come from unprejudiced and disinterested sources to carry any weight, and the "ex parte" story of Gov. Bradford hardly meets that requirement.